INTERSECTION

INTERSECTION

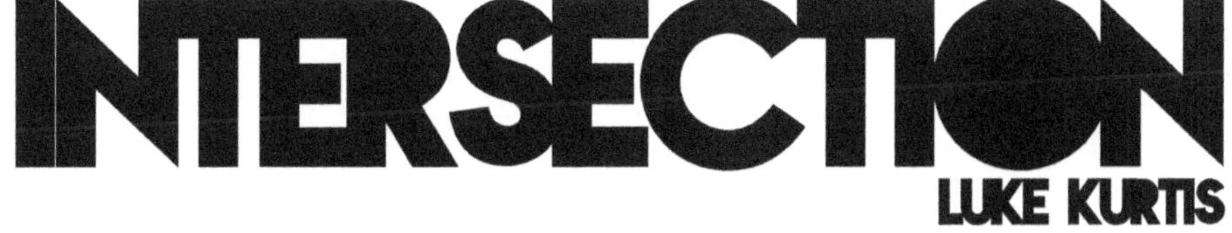

LUKE KURTIS

bd
nyc

The original limited edition of this book was published
on the occasion of luke kurtis's exhibition

INTERSECTION

8 March through 19 April 2014
at Massillon Museum/Studio M
121 Lincoln Way E, Massillon, OH 44646
www.massillonmuseum.org

The exhibition was made possible in part by the generous support
of Charlotte Jordan Griggs, Glynn & Julie Griggs, Michael D. &
Rhonda Scoggins, and Daniel P. Weick.

a luke kurtis/bd-studios.com production
published by bd-studios.com in New York City, 2016
Copyright © 2014, 2016 by luke kurtis.

Design by luke kurtis

ISBN 978-0-9890266-7-3 (trade edition)
ISBN 978-0-9890266-2-8 (limited edition)

hidden originally appeared in *Field Notes: Landscape and Architecture*
(Black Box Gallery, Portland, OR). "moment" originally appeared in *Red
Truck Review: A Journal of Southern Literature and Culture*, Mar 2014.
field and *cemetery* originally appeared in *Georgia Backroads*, Autumn
2013.

TABLE OF CONTENTS

"The [INTERSECTION] images function like metaphorical mile markers on a road trip to bridge what was once an emotional and psychological chasm between the rural *then* of kurtis's southern life and the *now* of his creative life in New York."

—Tom Wachunas, *ARTWACH*

"His landscapes are presented very unconventional and unusual. I like to be surprised. I see that in his work. He composes in such a way that it looks fresh, not like something you've seen 1,000 times before."

—Bradley Wilson
Creative Arts Guild (Dalton, GA)

INTRODUCTION

Southern culture is full of generations-deep traditions rooted in the surrounding environment. Growing up in the rural south is not easy if you don't fit the status quo. I moved away at such a young age—and there was a period of many years that I didn't return, not even to visit family. There were practical reasons for that, but there was also a conscious effort to distance myself. I didn't want to be southern.

By the time I returned to the south, I had gained a new perspective on the world. I was taken aback by the beauty of the southern landscape and the richness of its traditions. I couldn't believe I had grown up there. Looking back, I think the years away were necessary for me to appreciate and understand my roots. My vision was no longer clouded by previous negative experiences of the south. Time had healed old wounds, allowing me to see my homeland with a fresh perspective.

INTERSECTION is my ode to the south. These works show what I saw after going back there. I wanted to use my sense of artistry—what I see as a very "New York" part of myself—to expose an unseen side of the region. I knew I was touching on a different perspective when another Georgian native commented on one of my photos, "Who knew a squash plant could be art?"

And who knew my homeland—that place I once found so opressive—could be so beautiful?

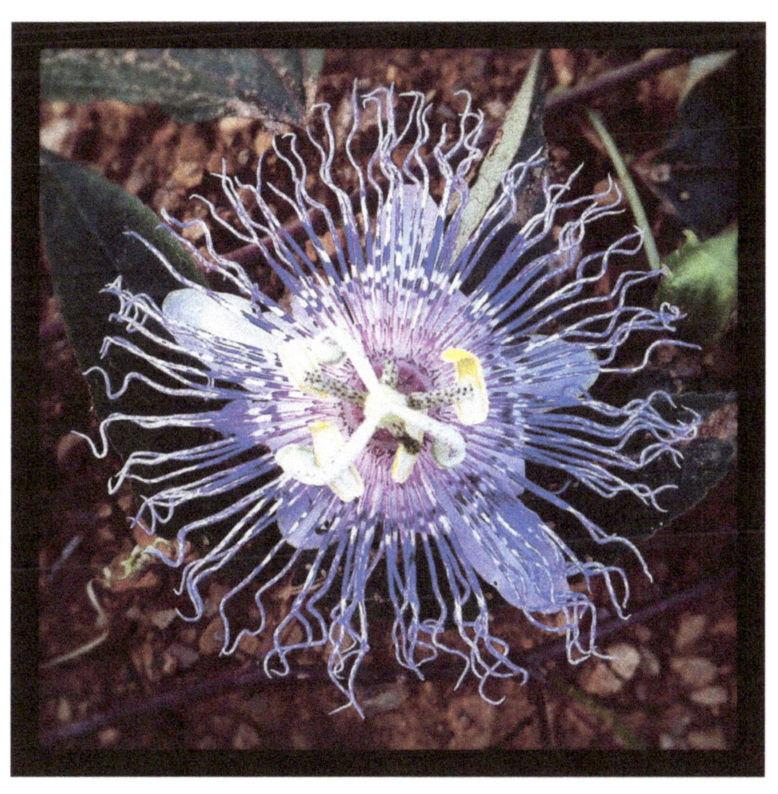

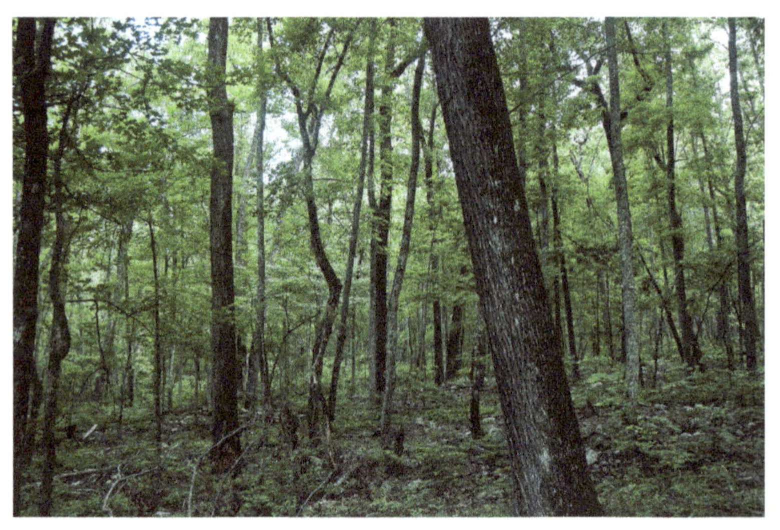

cherokee hills

was there ever a time
when the land was not scarred
our thoughts marred with violence passed
down by each generation?

did those cherokee hills
leave a river of blood
memory dredged in mud too dark for memory
and lost in translation?

when i think of home
there is joy but deep pain
and it's still the same all these miles back
with time running against you

now when do i go
this solemn exile, this trail of tears
so many years since i have been one
with that land. what are you to me?

when i look back i see
my dimming past ever more,
recollection is sore but no one else recalls
the cross i bear

it is mine alone
and no matter where i tarry
i always carry the sadness of the place
i call home

those cherokee hills
bear the soul of my name—
my heart is lame—my love in exile
set upon the path for a new tomorrow

for a pale horizon
a time soon forgotten fading fast
tradition passed down and slowing
like the decay of a quiet eruption

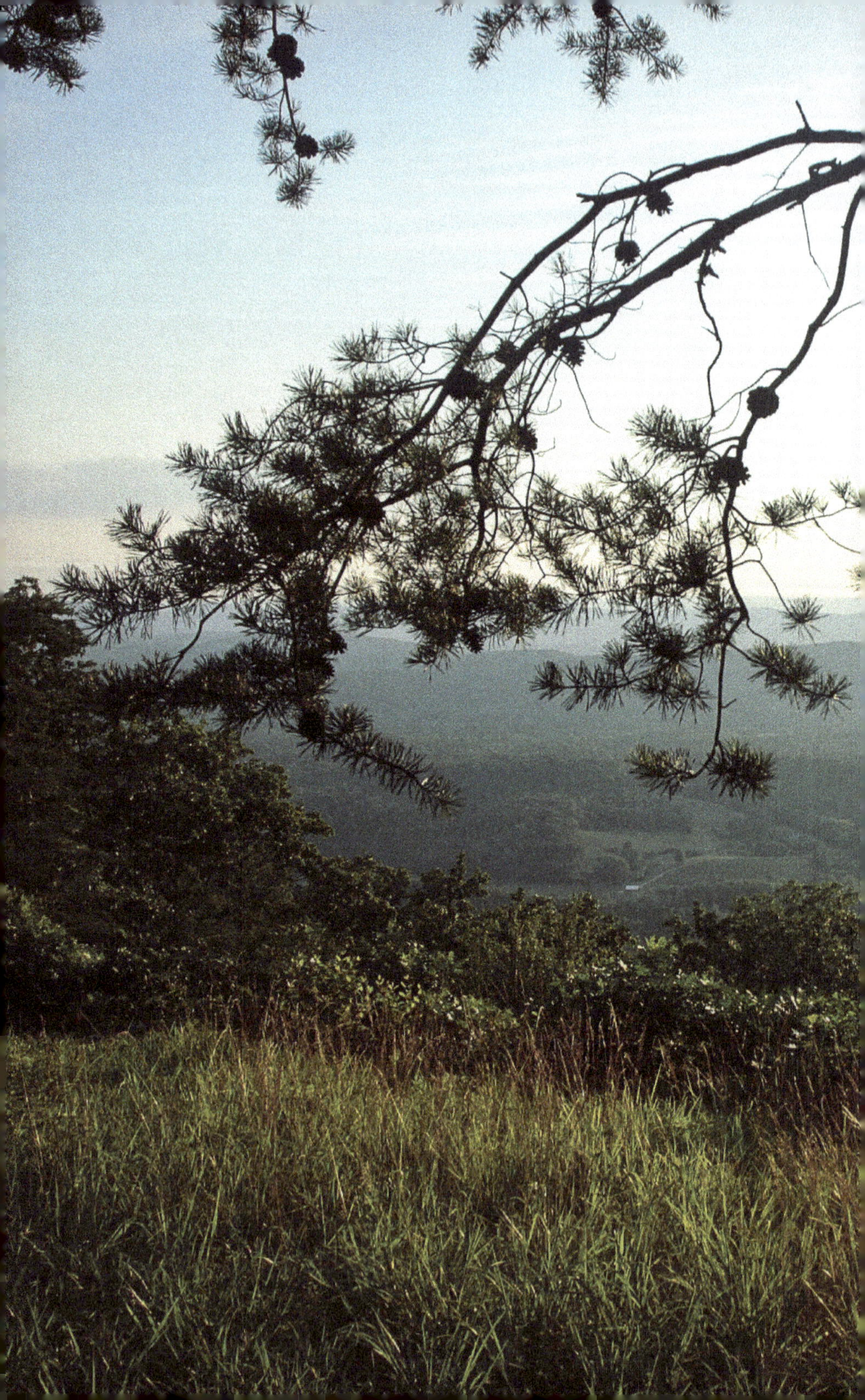

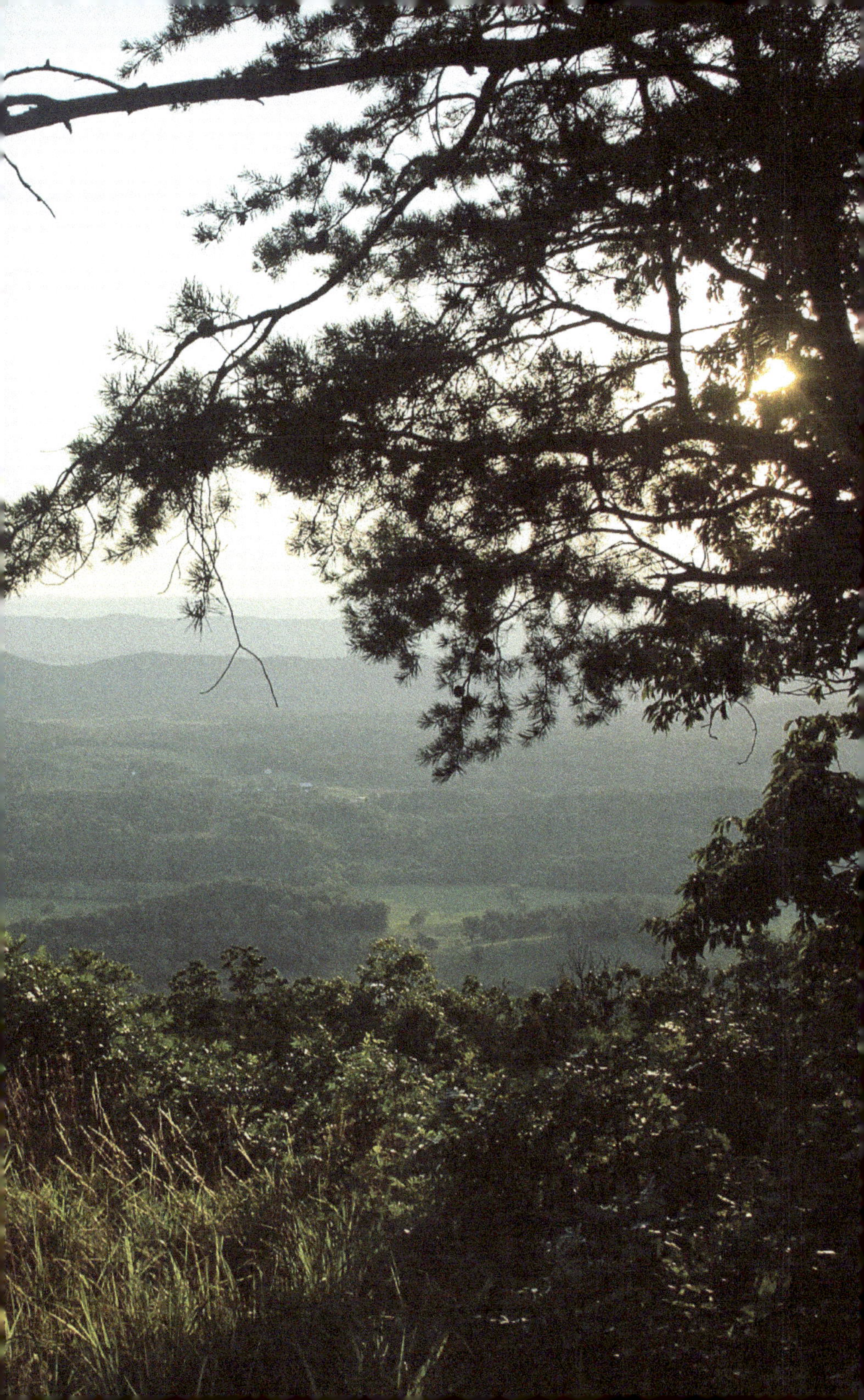

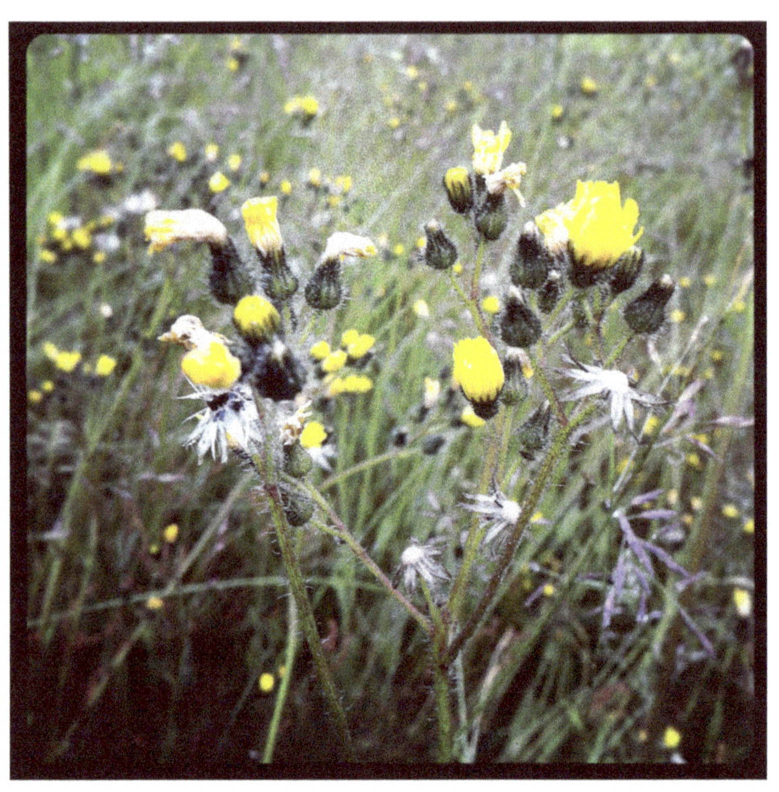

rambling journey

On Saturday morning July 25th I started on a rambling journey. When I left my home I didn't think of going very far, but as I passed through the fields, viewing the corn, cotton, melons, peas, grass and many other things that God is blessing us with, it inspired my mind and heart with many glorious thoughts so I went on. Passed over a small stream of water and then I very soon came to the foot of Johns Mountain. It seemed that old mother earth was dressed in green, tipped with yellow, red and purple. The thought came to me, shall this earth be called a veil of tears and all its hopes be compared to a weathered loath. Is happiness below but a fading vision?

As I neared the top of the mountain I could see other mountains on either side. Nature, Nature, Lessons for us if we knew how to get them. I stood and gazed with eager eyes the far away valleys and mountains and thought of that beautiful song 'The far away land.' Those lands, though seemingly far away, were very near to me for I dearly love this old land of ours.

I came around under some cliffs and saw on the huge rocks the beautiful flowers and ferns hanging from the steep part of the mountain. I could but think that nature is a honey drop by which the Lord sweetens the bitter cup of his people. Dear readers I some times think if we would only take the right view of what the Lord has done for us and is doing for us, it would lift our hearts upward in hope to him who has blessed us

with so many grand and noble things here on earth
and we would try henceforth, not only to say, but to
feel that our praise and sacrifices for God are as little
wild flowers that our blessed Saviour has placed on so
many hills and mountains.

Claudia Brown
13 Aug 1903
The Summerville News

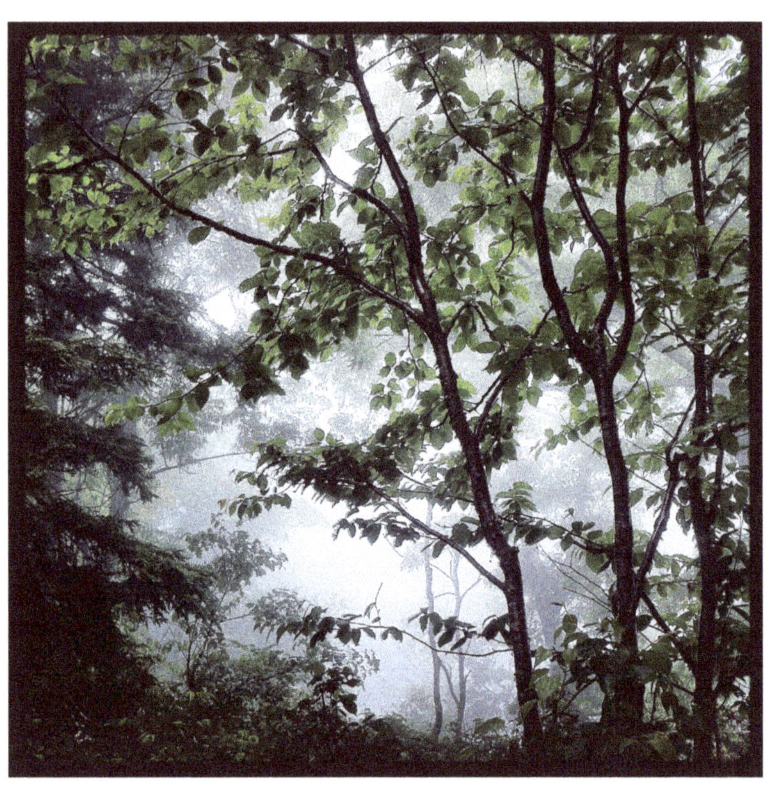

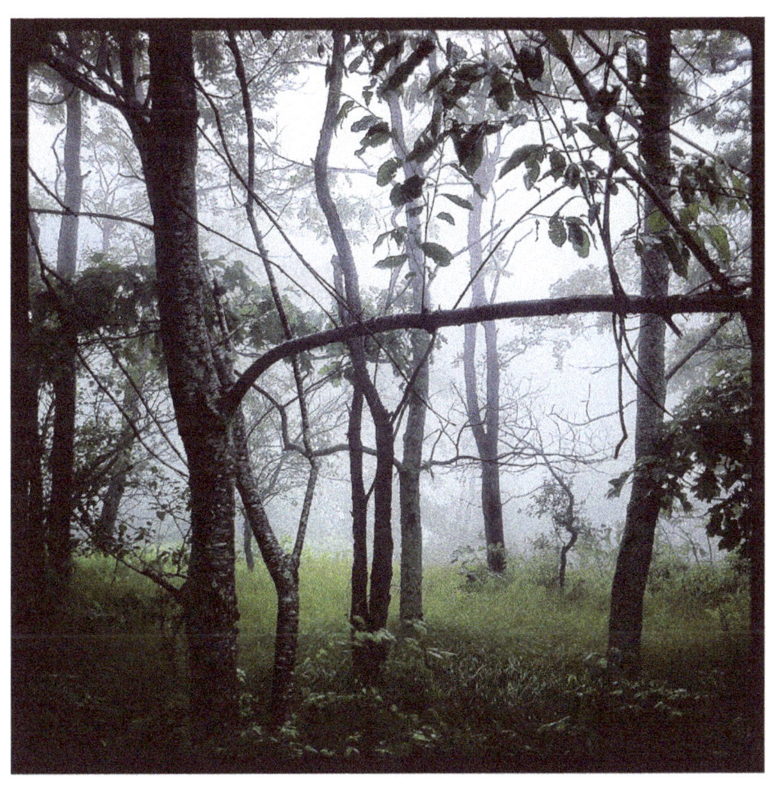

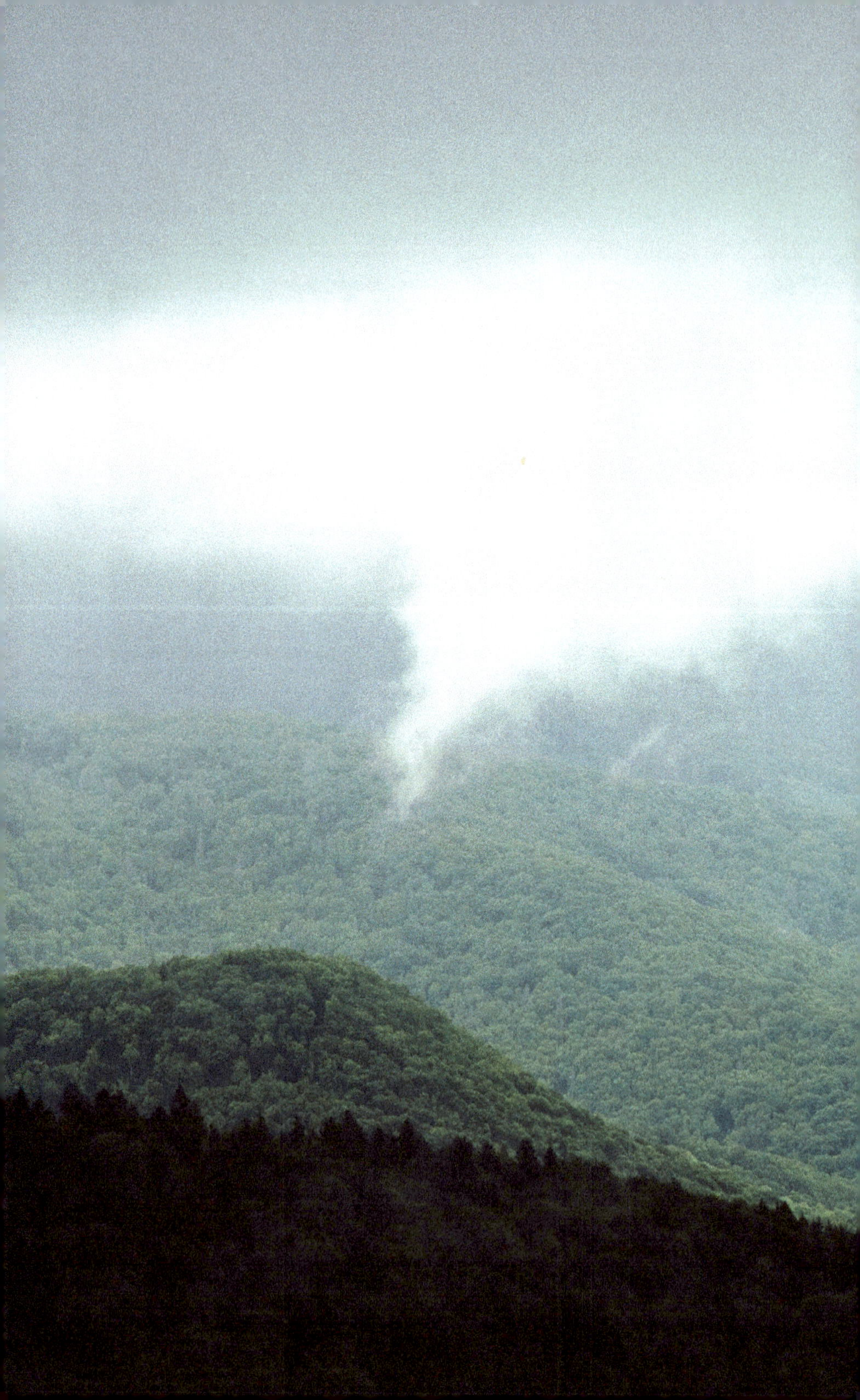

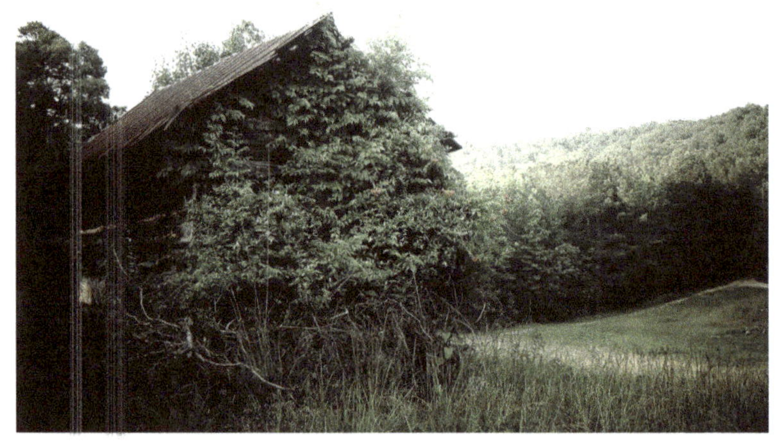

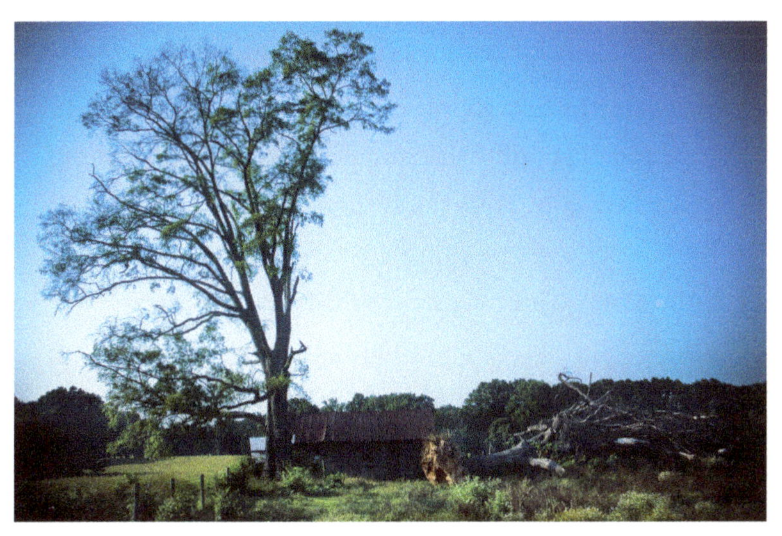

remedy

Will some one give me a remedy for fleas? Now I don't mean flee to take flight, I mean flea that takes a bite. The kind that will prize and scratch around your leg and when you go to catch them they are done gone. These insects are very numerous. Every body has some thing to say about fleas. Some say they are all over the woods. One fellow says that he had seen them sitting on a log pitching gravel at each other. Some one said that they were destroying C.L. Keith's potatoe patch. At any rate they are the worst I ever knew them in Georgia. You will find as good a remedy for your fleas in the following. Take a small bit of flea poison, catch the flea and choke it until it opens its mouth, then put some of the poison down its throat and you will find that by doing four or five this way that the balance will immediately "Get out."

12 July 1894
Walker County Messenger

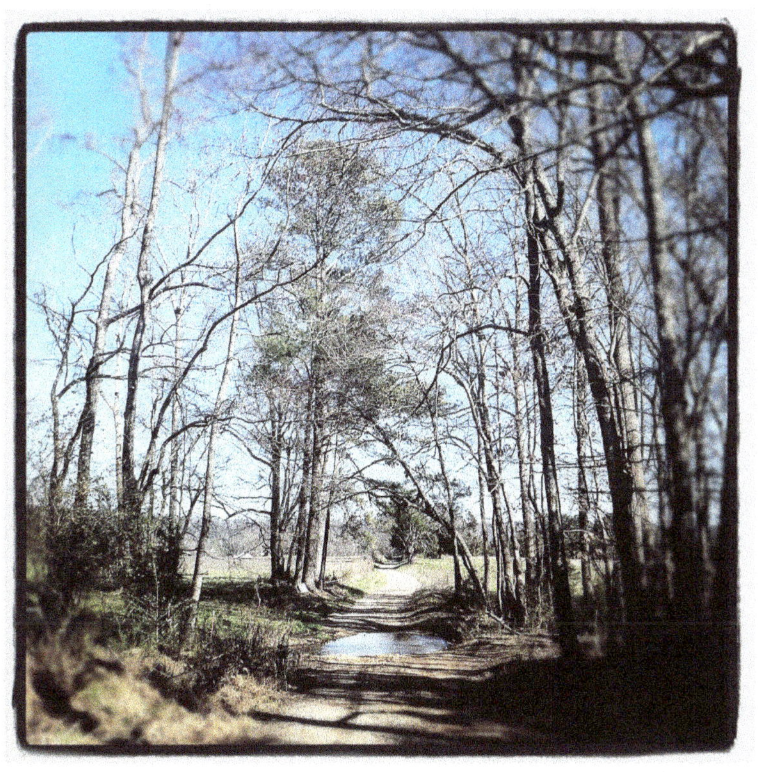

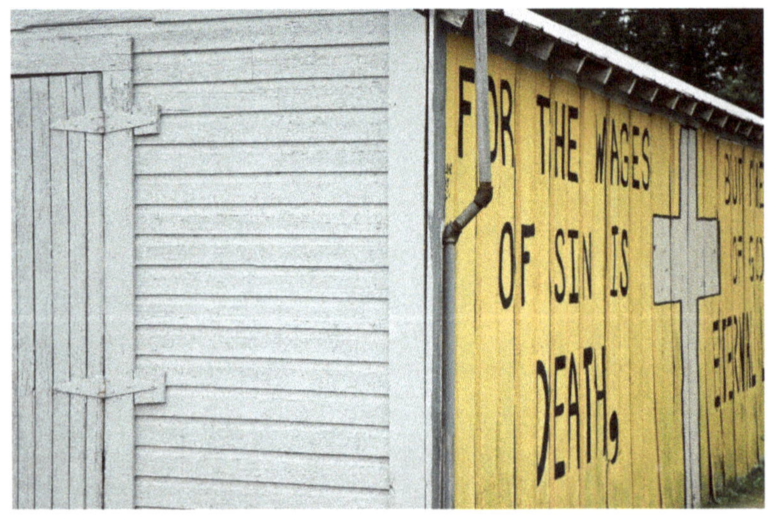
FOR THE WAGES
OF SIN IS
DEATH,
BUT THE
OF GO
ETERNAL

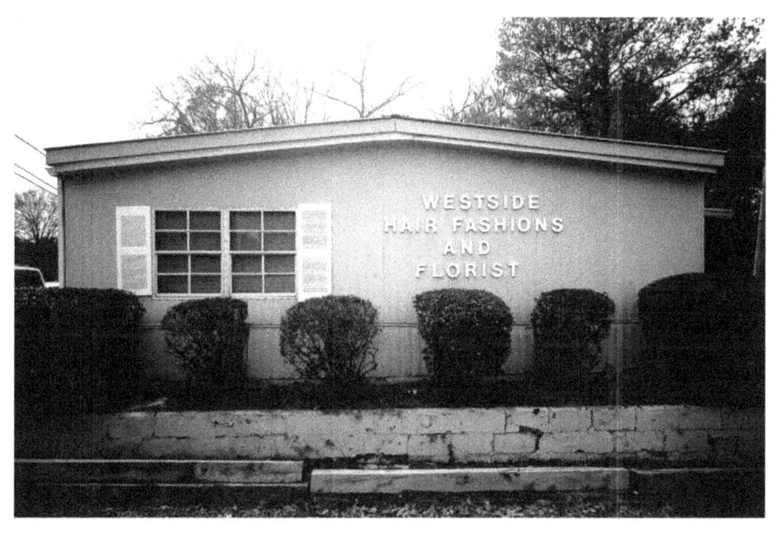

WESTSIDE
HAIR FASHIONS
AND
FLORIST

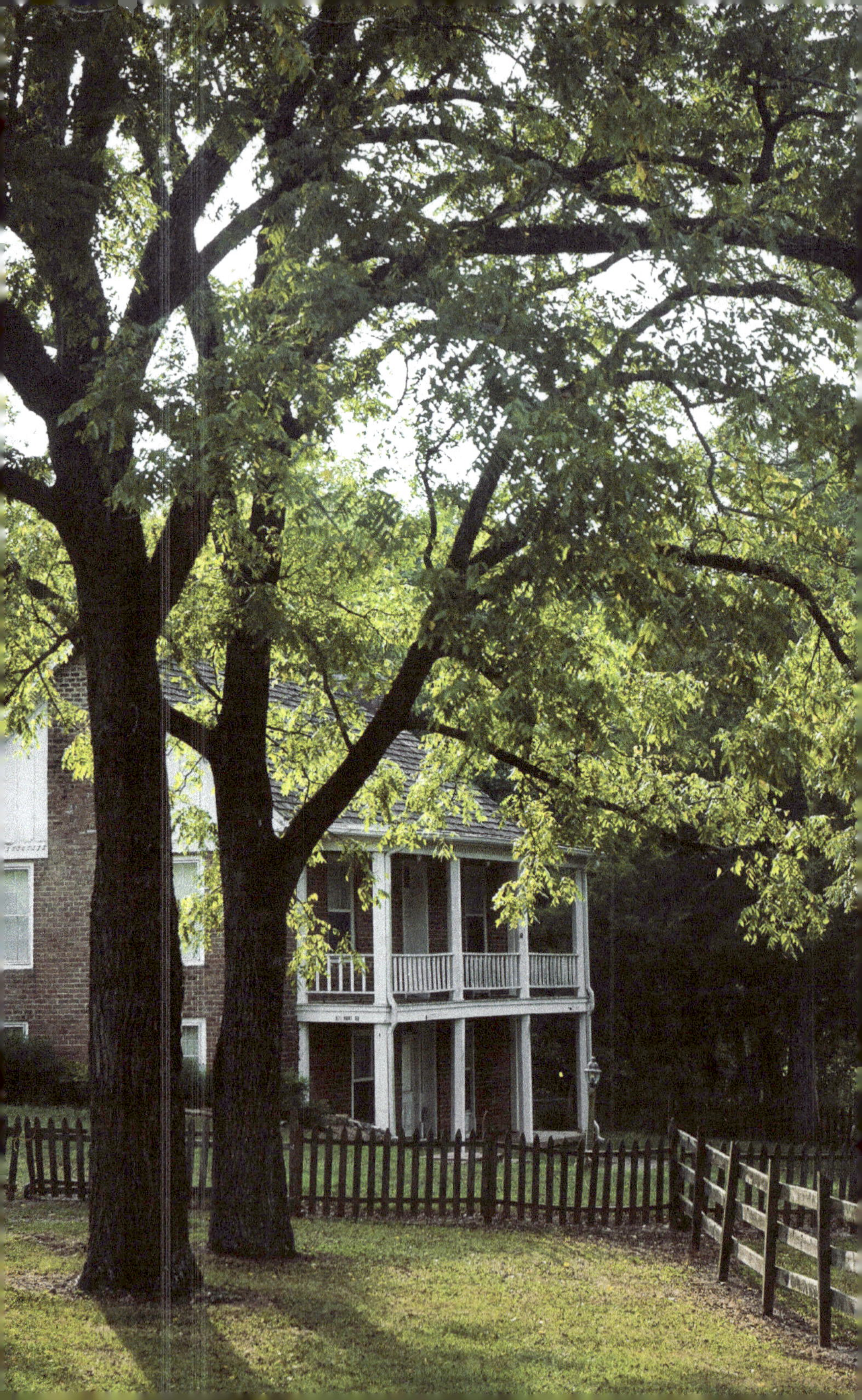

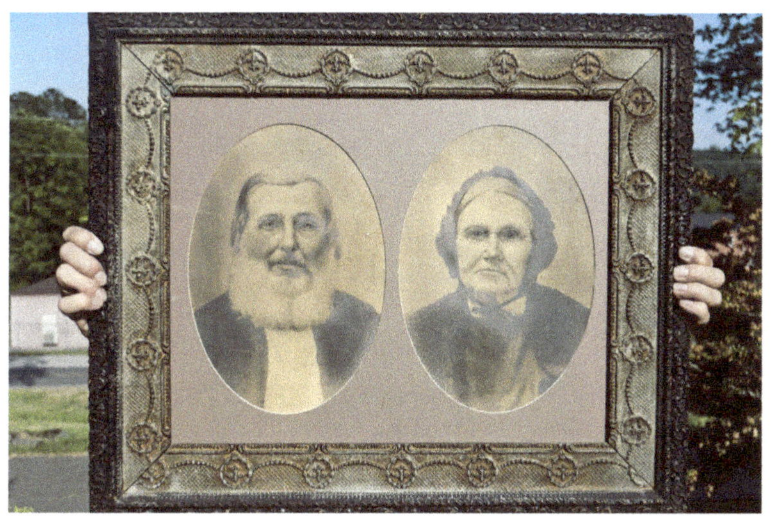

a gay and festive buck

John is a native of Dirt Town Valley, in Chattooga county, and withal a gay and festive buck. Having for some time breathed the air of the city and basked in fortunes smiles, John determined to pay a visit to the scenes of his boyhood. Now be it known that John dresses well. His clothes fit nicely and with his graceful equipoise; his linen is matchless in its snowy whiteness and marbleized smoothness. John determined to astonish the natives and he did. His tout ensemble was superb; the fragrance of Hoyt's German lingered around his jovinian curls and imperial. Now some of the boys of Dirt Town Valley thought they knew a thing or two because they had been to New York once and to Rome several times.

They gathered in knots around John upon his arrival, and gazed with rapture upon him. One said: "John, what did such a coat as that set you back?"

John replied with nonchalant air, "Well it is a cheap affair. I think it cost me a trifle—some $75."

"Gosh-darn-it-all" the crowd would exclaim "its dirt cheap!" while their eyes would dilate to the size of a saucer and their months would gape open.

"John, what did you pay for such pants?" was the next query.

"Well, they are only ordinary ones. They cost only $25."

"Them's fine shirts, John. How much did they cost?"

"Well, boys, I didn't expect to stay more'n a day or so and only brought along three dozen. I paid $36 a dozen for them. Nice, ain't they!"

And he was catechised in this manner throughout. John believed he had created a "sensation" and he had. Next morning as he passed down the street he could hear the boys shouting across the street to one another. "Say, Bill, I only brought down three dozen shirts and am only going to stay a day or two. I want to borrow a couple of dozen to make out a change."

John returned to the city much improved in physical vigor but he did not tell his city friends of this Idyl of Dirt Town Valley.

12 March 1875
The Atlanta Constitution

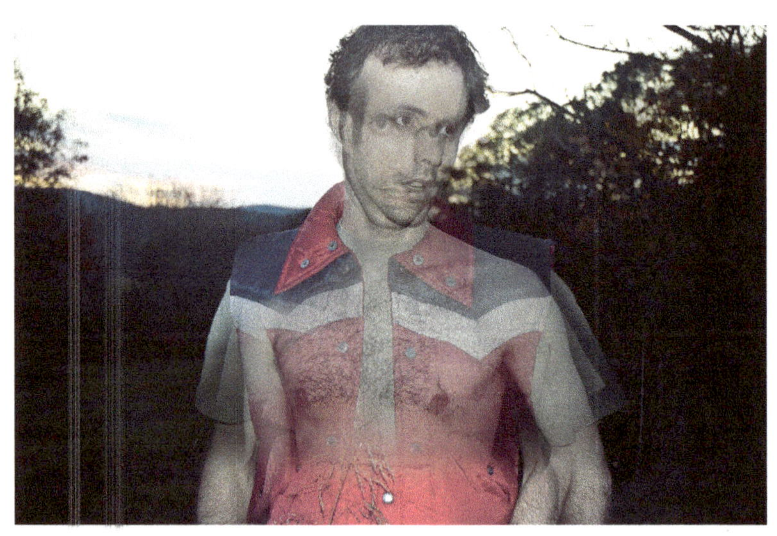

intersection (set the way towards heaven)

which parts are me?
and which did i imagine

who am i
really?

there's your
perception

and
mine

there's then
there's now

there's
the infinite

it's what's beyond
that matters

so where's
the intersection?

set the way towards heaven

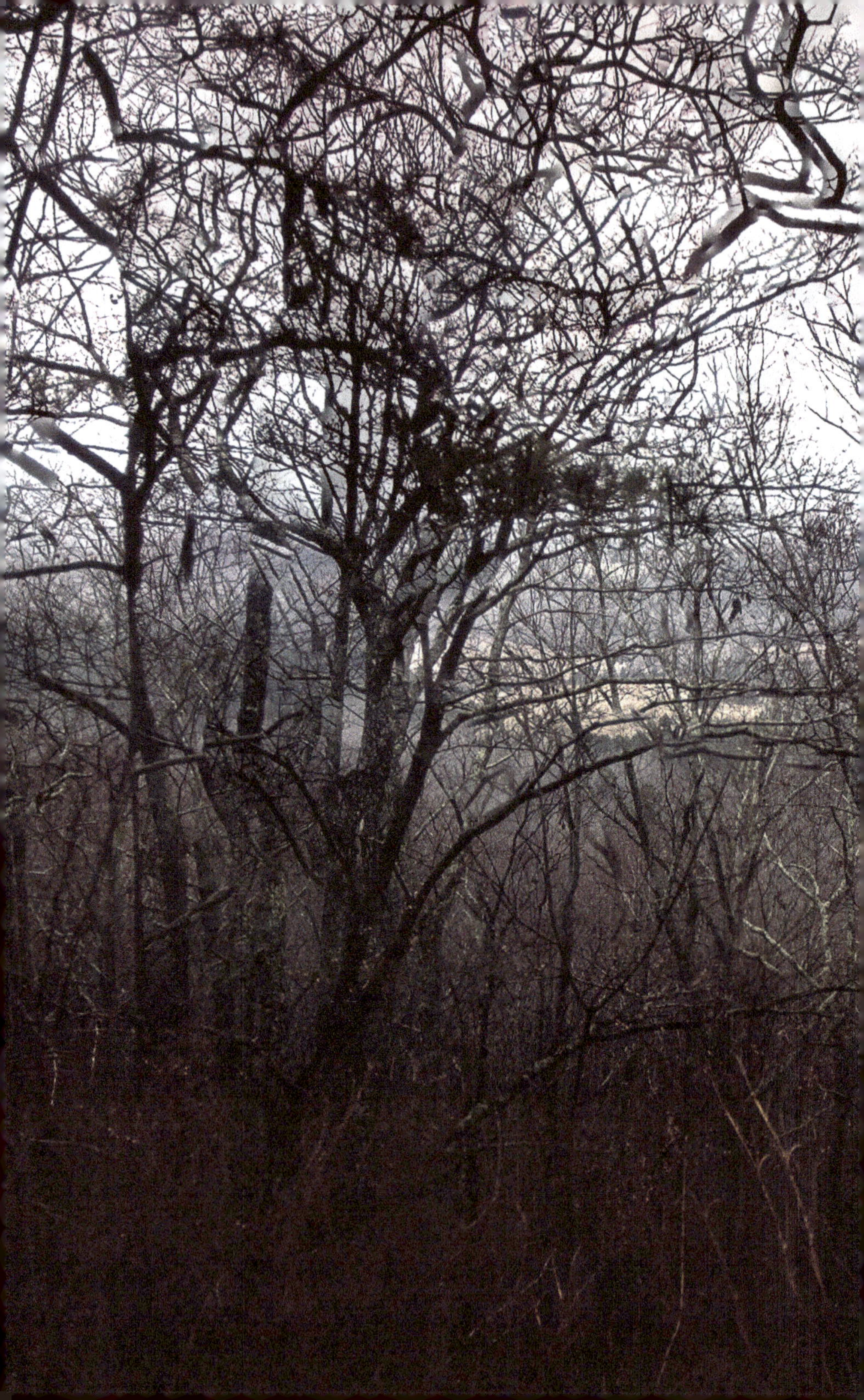

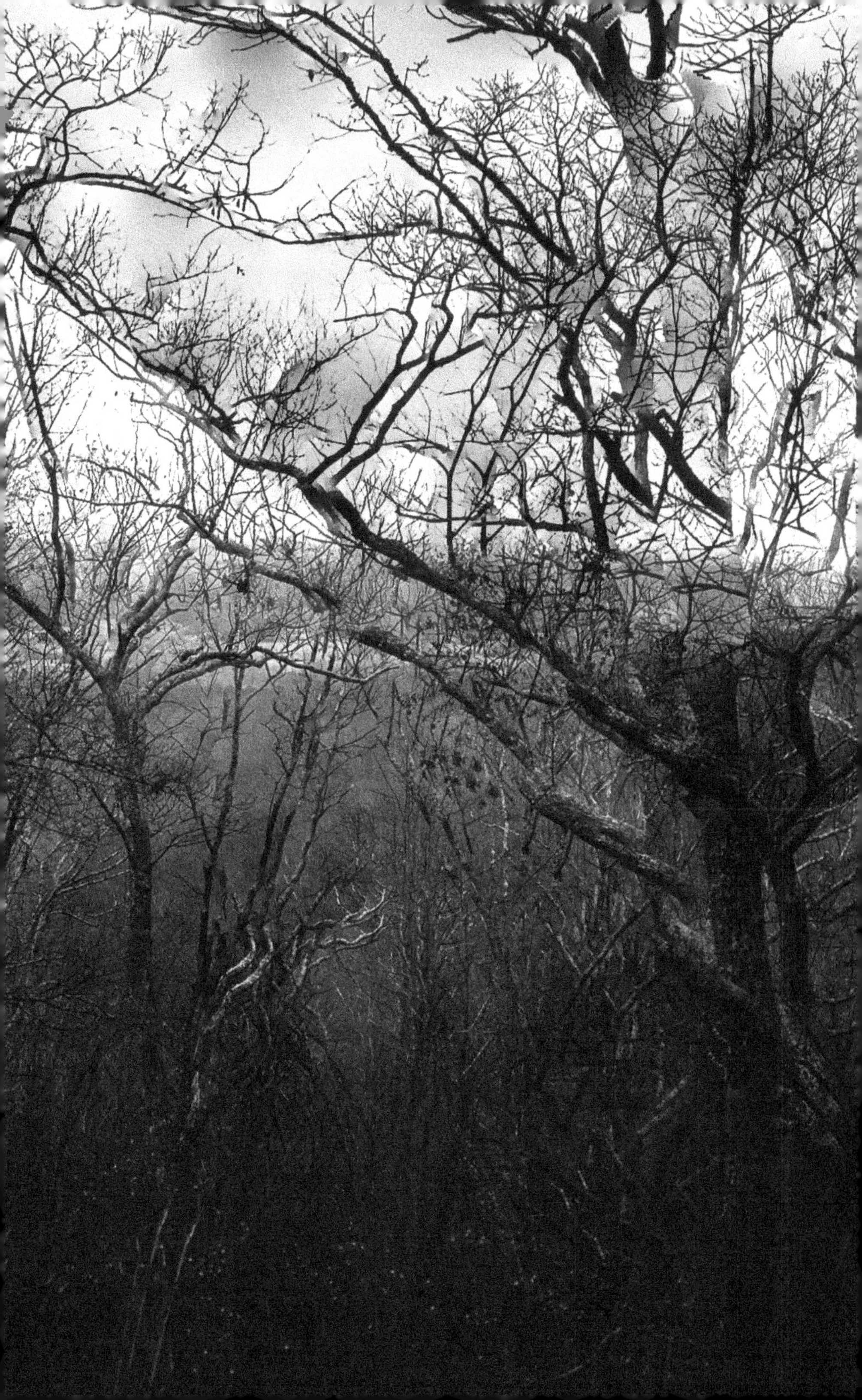

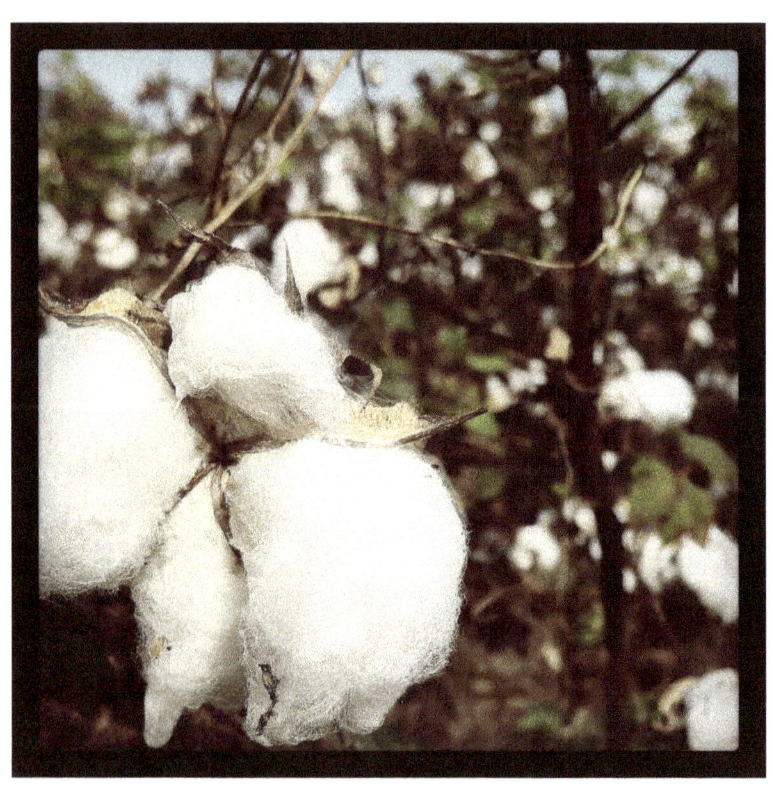

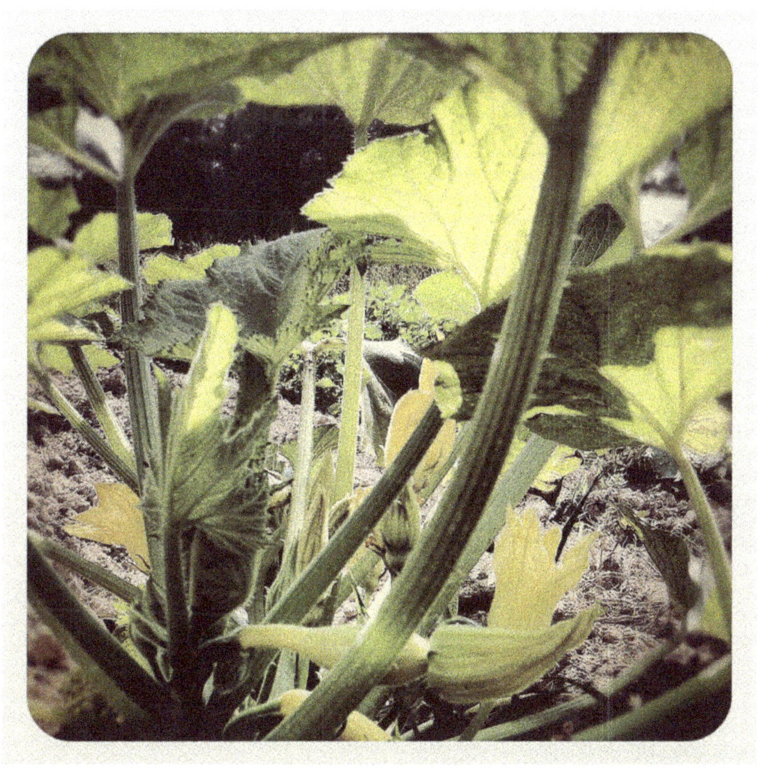

moment

if you want to know what life is,
i don't know what to tell you.
the answer's not in this city
or any other place i've been.
except maybe bell buckle tennessee
or new smyrna beach florida.

i haven't been to new smyrna in years
and bell buckle even longer!
though i'd like to visit again:
very nice places.
i don't recall the faces.
i never knew anybody there.
i just knew the earth.

bell buckle was quiet
a wide spot in the road
with about a million antique stores.
it was like rummaging through grandma's attic.
that's another place you might find
just what life is: in the attic.

new smyrna was my home
not home growing up.
it seems like i was born there.
when you get down
far south as new smyrna
the people start growing older
and lived most their lives up north.
no, in the north you won't find answers,
but you may find answers in the old.

i've learned secrets never told
and hearts who've never sang.
isn't that a shame?
no, not really, when you think about it.
you can't stop a heart from singing.
sometimes you may not hear it
but by god i know it's there.
everywhere.

villanow: home.
my georgia paradise.
i never found answers there
but i return often if only in my mind,
those green fields and dewy mornings,
the old swimming hole, the ancient trees,
that fertile valley, the messy red clay
caked between my fingers

yet the question lingers:

and if you want to know what life is,
i don't know what to tell you.

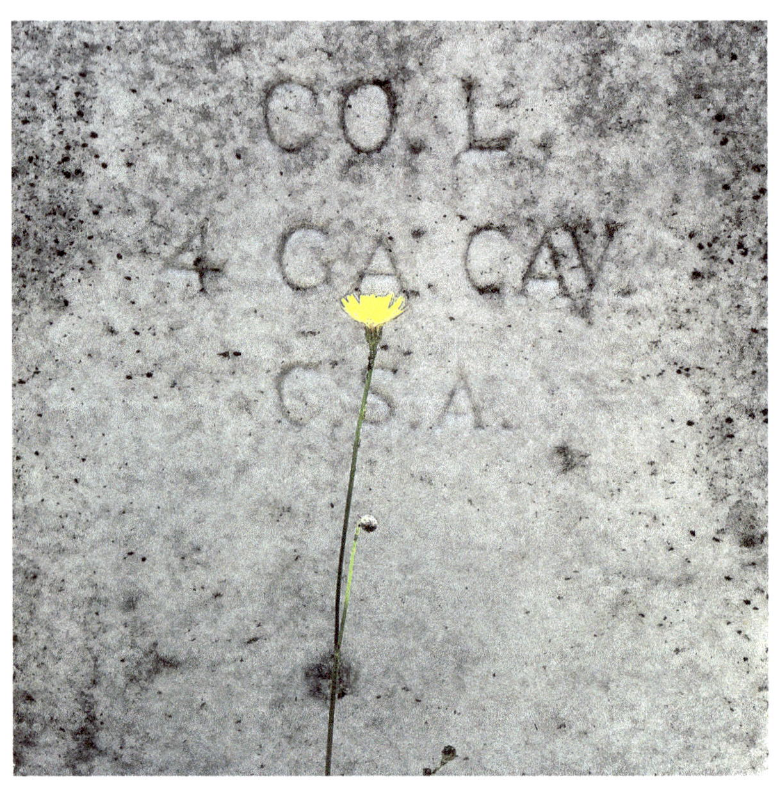

46

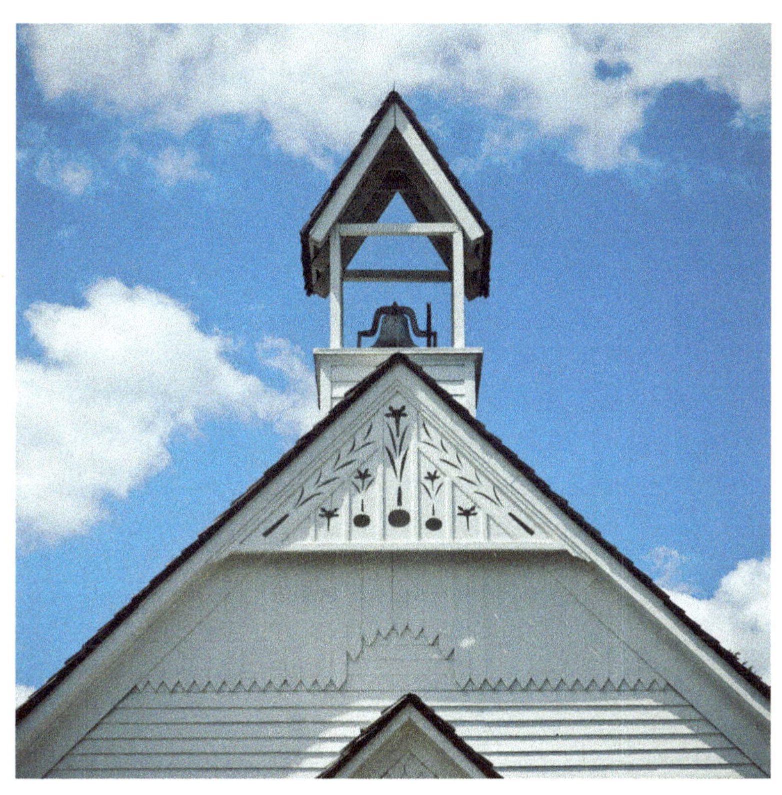

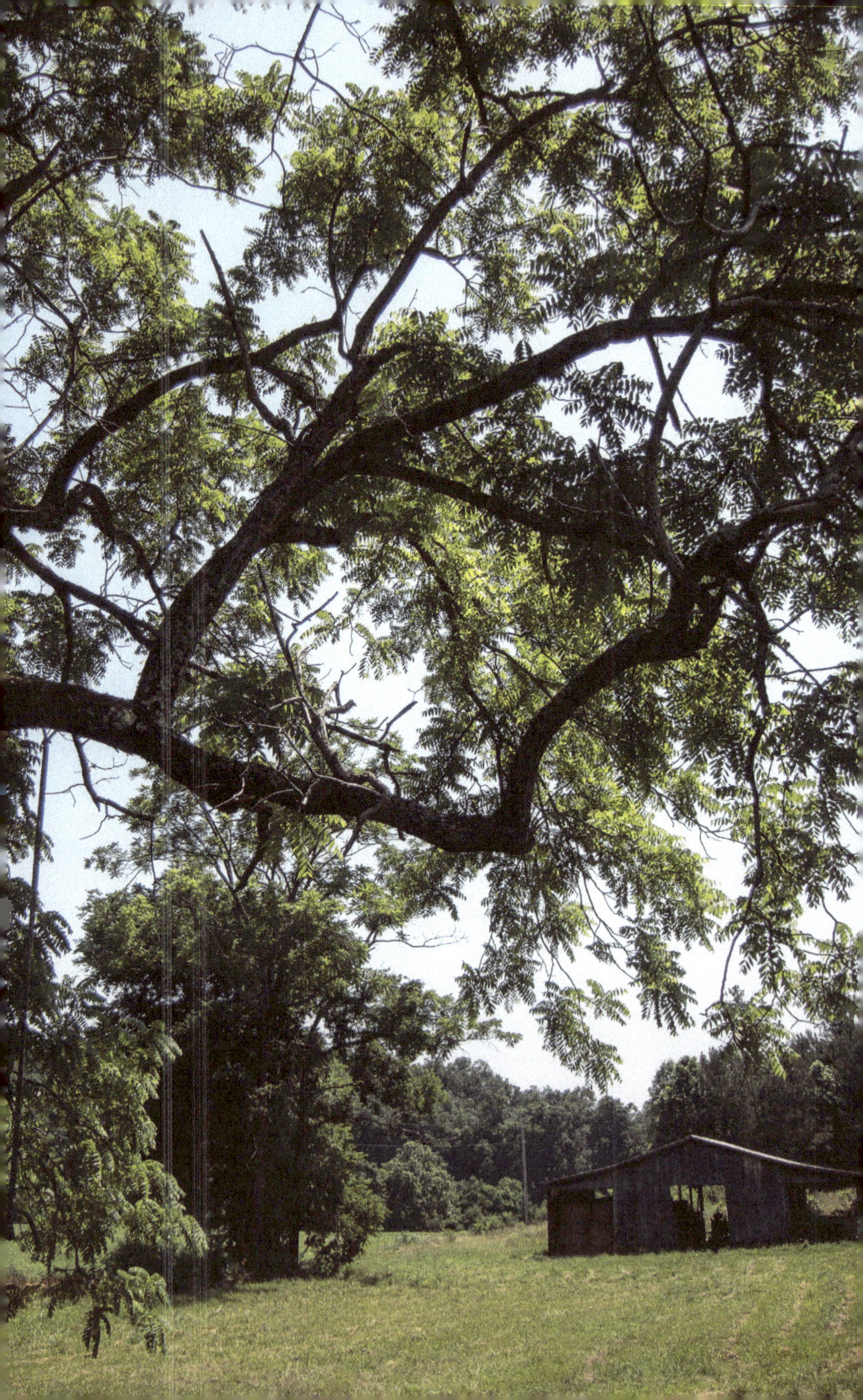

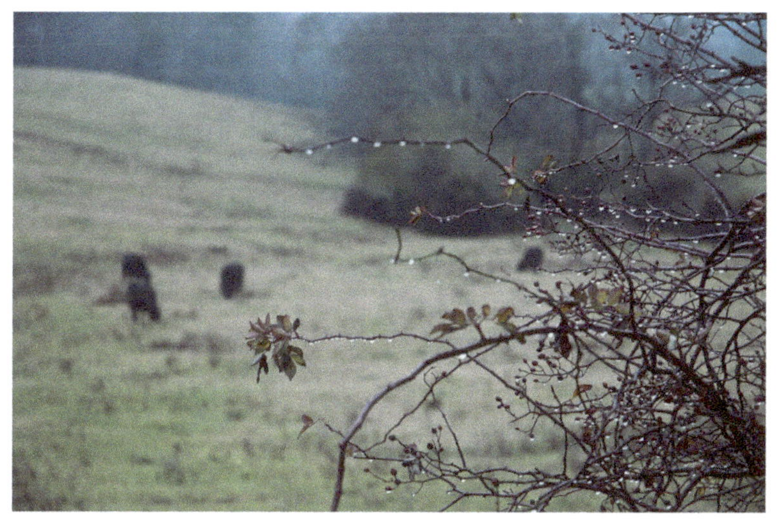

then came sweet rest

In December, 1864, my father got together the best available means for travel—wagons and one-seated buggy, all drawn by worn-out war horses, which were left us by the Yankee soldiers instead of the good ones they had taken from us. My father, with two sisters, Mary, Sarah, myself and some of the slaves, began the journey. We traveled twenty miles the first day. I walked the whole distance. We had to take it by turns riding, for there was not room for all to ride at once; but I chose to walk the whole day, I was so happy, going home!

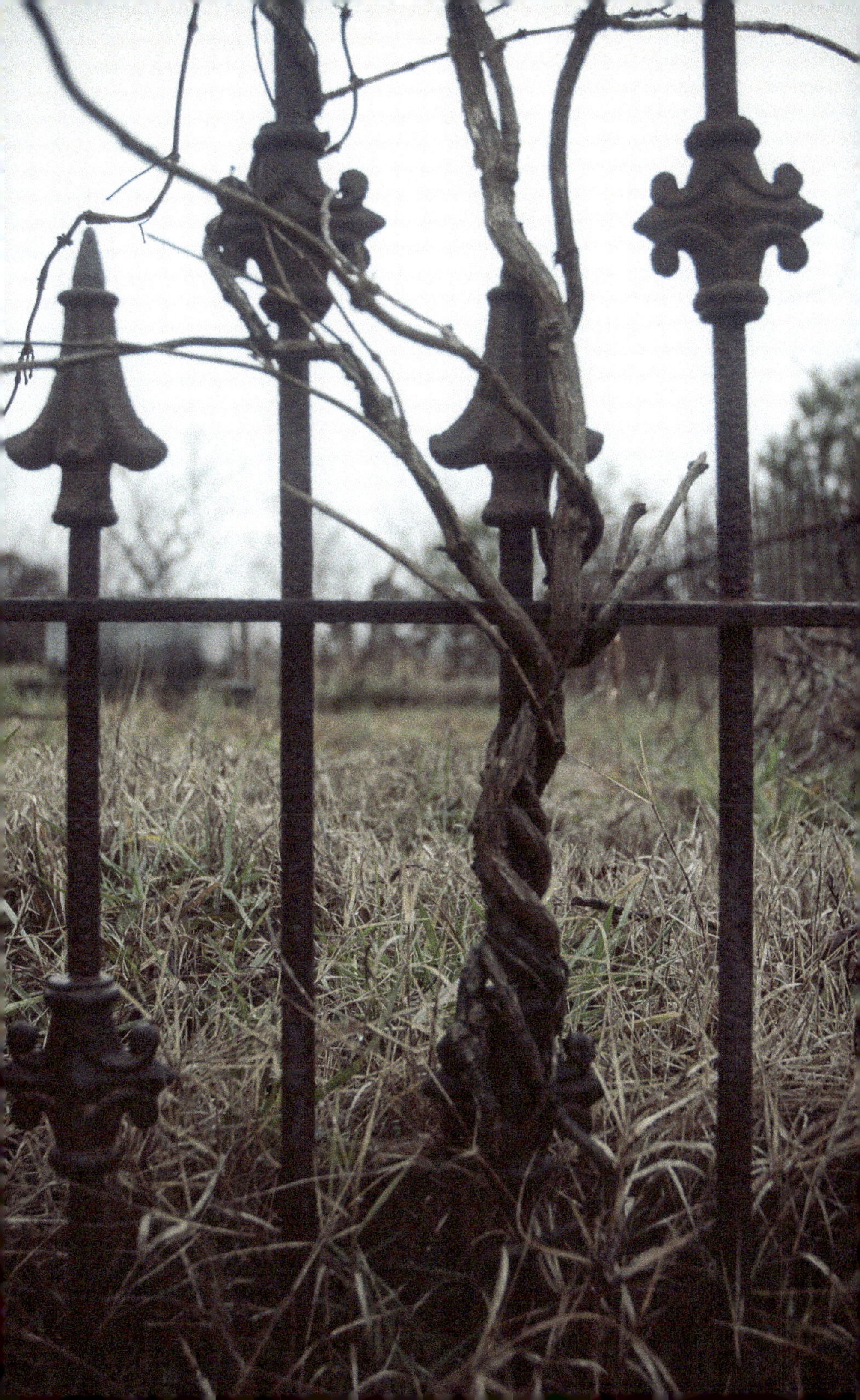

My father had a pair of shoes made for brother to wear to war but they were too small for him. I could wear them, though they were too large for me—they were made of rawhide—I was tired, heels and toes blistered, so next morning some other arrangements had to be made for the sore-footed little girl. The rickety old two-seated buggy, drawn by a scrawny little black mule, which could scarcely be seen over the dashboard, with harness that well matched, was lined up; I took the driver's place, six little negroes were packed in, one an infant, in my lap, and we started on the second day's journey. The sun shone brightly for three days; in the evening of the third day there were signs of rain; by morning it was coming down, and for the balance of the three weeks' journey old Sol hid himself. We did not stop for rain. Oh! the mud, the slush, the roads, the swollen creeks, beggar description—just imagine the worst and maybe you can get a faint idea of the conditions. My father would stretch the tents near some pine groves. After the tents were pitched, the ground was covered with branches from the pines; then the beds were made on top of these and a log heap fire was built at either entrance of the tents, then came sweet rest.

Dora Suttle Tittle
Sartain's *History of Walker County, Georgia*

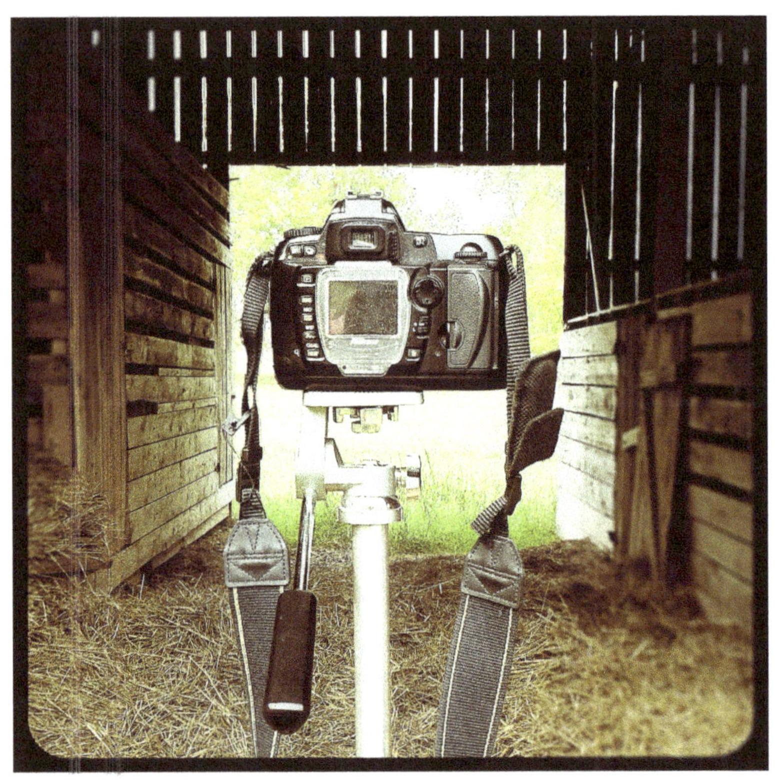

The photography and texts in this book were part
of the *INTERSECTION* exhibition at Massillon
Museum. The following installations were also part
of the exhibition.

everything laid out from beginning to end
but not necessarily in that order
2013/2014
Photocopied zines (endless copies), literature racks.

We Are One People
2013
Portfolio of 12 digital chromogenic prints
and 12 digital electrophotographic prints.

ABOUT THE ARTIST

luke kurtis (also known as Jordan M. Scoggins) is a Georgia-born interdisciplinary artist focusing on the intersection of photography, writing, and design. He has exhibited work in galleries and alternative spaces around the country. His debut solo museum exhibition, *INTERSECTION*, featured photography and writing and opened at Massillon Museum in March 2014. His multimedia project *Jordan's Journey* used genealogical and historical research as a device to explore the idea of personal and collective memory. Related articles and photography have appeared in *Georgia Backroads*. Other publications include the *INTERSECTION* zine featuring his original writing and art as well as his poetry collections *let us prey* (featured in RikArt Artist Book Collection, Rikhardinkatu Library, Helsinki, Finland) and *quilt*. His work has also appeared in *The Emerson Review, Encounters, Iceland Review, The Red Truck Review, Skin To Skin*, and *S/tick: Feminists on Guard*. In 2012 he co-founded New Lit Salon Press. He lives and works in New York City's Greenwich Village. Visit luke at http://bd-studios.com

Other titles published by bd-studios.com

Kissing Hedwig by luke kurtis
marie was an artist by luke kurtis
Visions of the Beyond by Stefanie Masciandaro
Tentative Armor by Michael Harren
The Language of History by luke kurtis
Retrospective by Michael Tice
Jordan's Journey by Jordan M. Scoggins